Remedies for
Disappearing

Remedies for Disappearing

Alexa Patrick

Haymarket Books
Chicago, Illinois

Published in 2023 by
Haymarket Books
P.O. Box 180165
Chicago, IL 60618
773-583-7884
www.haymarketbooks.org
info@haymarketbooks.org

ISBN: 978-1-64259-913-8

Distributed to the trade in the US through Consortium Book Sales and Distribution (www.cbsd.com) and internationally through Ingram Publisher Services International (www.ingramcontent.com).

This book was published with the generous support of Lannan Foundation, Wallace Action Fund, and the Marguerite Casey Foundation.

Special discounts are available for bulk purchases by organizations and institutions. Please email info@haymarketbooks.org for more information.

Cover design by Rachel Cohen. Cover artwork: "And We Begin to Let Go" by Njideka Akunyili Crosby © 2013. Photo credit: Jason Wyche, courtesy of the artist, Victoria Miro, and David Zwirner.

Library of Congress Cataloging-in-Publication data is available.

10 9 8 7 6 5 4 3 2 1

For my "Vigilante Aunties"
Geraldine, Lou, Pat, Willa, Betty, and Connie

Contents

You can't kill me, I was born dead.
—*Big L*

We dance at funerals; we got this.
—*Big Freedia*

Critical Missing II

for runaways

Bless us girls, apostrophes in our names;
hung drawbridges for the missing
continent in our chests, last seen
bowing behind the Atlantic. Since, time
has continued to chasm our contact,
dressing clear intention as American incident

(but these voids are no incident),
I've learned as I've attempted to name
the acute hurt: the desire for contact
without flinch, the mere warmth missing
from every greeting. Can't remember a time
when I was not chosen last.

I scour for myself in final
scenes, every happy ending incident
to my silent work, yet so many times
I disappear, unnamed
in the credits. If I take my missing
into my own hands, have no contact

with the world that abuses contact,
perhaps I will have a self that lasts. Seen
so many girls with my face go missing
as if we aren't the beauty incident
on the world's dull surface, their names
phantom amethysts embellishing time.

So I run so fast that even time
strains in its reach, struggling to contact
who it once held by the neck, by the name.
I breathe easier now. I was last seen

drawing wings on my chalk outline. Incidentally,
what tried to kill me missed.

A sad truth: sometimes we go missing
just because we've witnessed over time
how no one looks for us no one inciting
riots on our behalf. We: our only emergency contact.
This country: our emergency. We see
it smile as it buries our names.

Call it an incident when we go missing,
but remember our names. For we will return like time
to make contact with this dirt, before washing our feet in the sea.

1

Ode to an Almost First Kiss

He was one of the only
Black boys in school,
older, an athlete.

I, seventeen, unkissed, and waiting
on the beach and now
a better time than ever
to learn what my friends
have been telling me for years.

We watched waves spill onto the sand.
The sand drank the waves' clumsy offering,
my wanting making a mouth
out of everything.
Even the moon laughed at us,
two kids whose skin mimicked its sky.

He fumbled enough to create a tide
and broke as he told me
he preferred the light shore
of my friend's skin instead.
My disappointment was
swallowed by ocean.

He was not the first or only
boy to leave me buoyed.
The one before him was
anonymous valentine and
with no lighthouse to guide me
I spent my freshman year
guessing his name.

The one after him was a
dark corner at a party.

He touched me on purpose, then
walked by me in hallways
without saying a word.
I, unable to look at him
without tasting salt.

For a Black girl in my town,
you learned the worth of your body
by the number of boys who
wanted you, but didn't ask you out.
My color, clandestine,
unworthy of public sparkle,
the kind that dances
on the surface of The Sound.

As a Black girl in my town,
you dance on your own,
shame your body for wanting
anyone to touch it, validate it;
your dignity and humanity,
colliding horizons that
create sharp reflections
of yourself.

All I wanted was to look in
the mirror and be soft.
Even glass thrown into the sea
takes 30 years to be beautiful,
but for me, waiting like
giving all my edges
to undeserving hands.

With this boy, I was happy
just to have hands that looked like my own.

Maybe then, his, more willing to hold on,
though still, like always, the ocean
releases and releases.

And I wonder what moon
these boys were tethered to?
What shattered images of themselves
did they see as its light burned
their surface?
How bright that it blinded them
as I disappeared in my own dark?
Too Black to shine,
too Black to move a body,
pull it in close, I learned
Black girls have no gravity
to overwhelm a heart.
Even if the boy's skin, too, like tarred sky,
forgetting me makes him feel mighty,
an ocean, and I drowned
without ever touching him.

My mother once flattened my father's tires

because my father
kept driving on the grass
after my mother
told him not to.
Only a few months
after the divorce finalized, she,
anticipating disobedience,
delicately placed 11 nails
on the barren area
and awaited our return.

I still hear
the rusted words crowd
rental cars, swell
enough to drown
Stevie Wonder cooing
A Time to Love.

       I knew
       those sporadic weekends,
       Toys 'R' Us sprees,
       large pizzas,
       had deeper roots
       yet to surface,
       each feeling more apology
       than play, my father's face
       a drought, the lack of sleep,
       something running him
       over.

My mother was just fine.
Wanted my father gone, but
the lawn to keep
the flowers he planted.

Bulbs knotted, stubborn
fists refusing to sprout or
take direction.

She took consequence
into her hands,
tilled it with green thumbs,
tells the story to this day
behind laughter, saying

See, Baby, women in our family
know how to make angry men
listen, stop, or leave
without asking
twice.

       When he drove us back,
       after our two days
       at the Sheraton,
       after swimming pools,
       movies, a small vacation
       from a home
       to which he never
       fully returns,
       the air was thick as his
       stalled goodbye.

       Every time he did,
       my brother and I grew
       taller, like weeds, he said,
       mourning what he
       could no longer tend to,
       had only half of,
       a garden of grief
       pressed at his skin.

Again, he dropped us off,
ran over the grass,
backed out
of his once-driveway.

Shaking her head,
my mother watched him
try to resow
what power he had,
then leave, confident,
like she wouldn't
eventually
make her point.

One Time, the Aunties Made Lamb for Joe Morton

After the play, the sisters
swarmed him like flies
to melting candy or mushrooms
to wet earth, flashing
their frills

And he did not mind
cuz the metronome of their heels
made any man forget his long day
staining his collar and remember
the wide chest beneath

And the sisters? *Whew!*
Were walking eyelashes,
if the color pink could sing,
decorated demands in lace
before he even noticed
he was exactly where
they wanted,
sitting, hungry

Husbands off somewhere
in their Saturday, cigar
leather-thick basement
where they'd loosen ties and tongues
expect wives to wait, obey

But obedience was for homely girls,
not the six of them, leaning
into this handsome celebrity
like stems in a tall glass
before they had to return
to the quiet business of Sunday

They smiled, purled in a twang
that, too, knew the Bible by heart

Baby, what is your favorite meal?

The Groomsman

for Ralph

The story goes: he had a temper.
Curdled his fist into sharp prayer,
boiled saliva at the back of his throat.
Thought every officer was the officer
who swole his mama's face.

Everybody called him cousin.
He had a smile mamas
wanted to fatten. Maybe
smelled like sweat and peppermint
after a shift driving the truck.

He cleaned up nice, though,
casket sharp, cuttin'
niggas a 20 when they needed.
                    Thanks, man.
And maybe
a smaller version of my father
walked away thinking about groceries.

I imagine him fixing my father's
collar before the wedding.
Stained glass breaking
his strong jaw to soft colors.
Corner store god,
shattered ceramic
skin, shaded, foreshadowed.

They took his name,
frisked the clean Black
of his suit, adorned
his precious neck,

in a bowtie of bullet.
Oh, how the doves fled!

A week after his brother tied the knot,
the officers did too.

The Black Men outside the Waterfront Safeway

are a steady ballet of hands,
cipher of dab and dozen
transform southwest street corner
into Carnegie Hall.

I walk by. They quiet,
shield me from what profanity
fills the gaps in their teeth,
those golden smiles, the slick
tongues that make them.

Some trickle in across 4th
defying oncoming traffic.
Hood Moseses knowing
they control the wave.

Every day, no matter
the time, they gather
by gum-addled cement,
overflowing trash bins,
neglected memorial benches,
just to see each other—

A remedy to whatever else
might disappear.

Betty

We took the annual Pittsburgh procession down for a visit.
Our matching purple shirts made us bruises, bright & bringing
new drama to the hospice where Betty's life tapered like linen.

We'd pour our August gospel into the rec room, half-circled
at the center, where the nurse rolled her in. The skin of her face, thin
as lace, through which her gray eyes asked their cool questions.

Aunt Betty, once as loud as her sisters, now called their names
without speaking, wept at all these faces of hers, knocking like
neighbors
from past lives, holding her fragile hands, their bent scripture of
bone,
to kiss into them a safe passage.

& I, who never heard her voice, who only met her through my
mother's stories,
was too afraid to join in the hymn the rest of my family sung
& wondered
                    where all her noise went.

A Portrait of My Mother in Front of the Vanity

By 12 years old, she directed the choir.
Named her second album *This Is Love.*
Went on Broadway.
Had me harmonizing "My Little Sunshine" at 3.
Did backgrounds for Ray Charles, Aretha, Nick Jonas. Sometimes
I turn on the TV, hear her soprano
over a Walmart commercial—
her voice, everywhere.

She'd return home, perch at her distressed vanity,
remove The City from her face, as an entire world
of smoke and sweat shook from her braids.

When she couldn't find a sitter, she'd bring us along.
MetroNorth trained me to sit still. Sometimes
they'd even put me in the booth, and I'd get $100 for humming
on tune like she taught me. My mother—

who's been flirted with in Italy, stared at in Greece,
who gave me glamorous aunties dressed in big sunglasses,
deep lipsticks, black clothing, who makes a living of being listened
to—
often gets tired of all the noise. Asks me to turn off the radio.
She nods to silence as if it were a song.

Geraldine Sees Her Dead Mother from the Kitchen Window

She was sick but still
cleaned tirelessly,
attended to her children's
eager mouths, kissed
her husband's stoic face,
watching, dutiful,
as they devoured
her daily work.

Each day brimmed
with more mess to solve.

Her favorite drama:
hours alone at the sink
when light finally coughed
its last breath through
the kitchen window,
a glowing goodbye dripped
against faded wallpaper,
transforming her kitchen
into a new life!

So ordinary each day.
That day.
She barely noticed
her decades-passed mother
sitting outside
the torrid pane,
below the willow,
picking her teeth
with a loosed twig.

mommy? she said in the voice
of a little girl just waking up

MOMMY! Now with an authority
that startled her.

[no answer]

The wind gathered her skirt,
a smile, almost, waving
behind her black eyes.

Gone too soon, yet infinite,
they both stayed there
looking at each other
like two mirrors.

Geraldine's Elegy

Before MS jammed the doors,
and cancer rotted the floorboards,
she housed mischief

Crossed her eyes
during grandpa's sermon,
bit tomatoes, whole, like apples

That kind of unruly cannot be buried
without it growing into someone else

I was two when my mother
lifted me to her face,
called out her own mother's name
just to see which one of us
would respond

I am the most like her when
I am somewhere I shouldn't be

Death, nothing
but another thing
to abandon

I mourn someone
whose face I have.
My grief, a disobedience

Talk with my mouth full
of her, tilt my head
toward the sky
stick out my tongue

Sugar

Gathered like sunflowers
at the breakfast table,
six sisters share a midnight,
wash down 7UP cake
with the kind of laughter
reminding you they are
in the choir,
bells in their throats
like hallelujah,
the sweetest thing.

This, before their hands cracked
from prayer and spanking babies,
when they'd pinch blood
into their cheeks,
fix the lipstick which gracefully
announced the small mole
they all kept at the corner
of their mouths. So pretty,
even their sharpest words
were frosted.

I come from sugar
the way a hymn comes
from grief or praise.
I have so many ways
to return:

grease my scalp with the same oil
I use for pans and find myself
in a Pittsburgh kitchen,
forget everyone's name
and weep because I love them,
dream of pistols under pillows,

wake up bitter about husbands
I don't yet have. Every morning,
a manicured finger
pointing home.

Grandma Gerry went first.
Winked at my mother
from the casket.
Aunt Willa passed
on her 102nd birthday.
They all know how to make an exit,
make us mourn in confection.

Grace, not dead,
heirloomed,
like beauty mark or
recipe, there even
in the cavities left behind.

Their stories coat my teeth;
I, too, am beside them.
Never alone or lost, just alive,
with their names trailing
like crumbs to God.

2

"Too Much"

when held right it is a weapon

and i am fourteen again
thighs already rubbed holes
in the good jeans
bright red braces, offensive
making stop signs of every tooth
stretching gaps until my mouth
is more machine than human

when i smile
wielding both rows of teeth
wear the clothes the rest of me
has not yet swallowed
the pale-necked boys
the ponytail-pendulum girls
cringe at the gesture's persistent grind

i have since only attempted quiet
allowed my limbs a smaller radius
became subtler target
but my eyes are loud with their dark
hair curls, obnoxious
everything about me claps

Can something vast be wounded?
            No–a bullet in the sky
            is only a warning–
smoke, like futile breath, wheezes
out the barrel:

Look!Your hair sticks out!Look!Your purple elbows!Your fat thighs!Look!

i mighty myself
let my joy bark, uncross legs
laugh until even the hurt burns

i'm so big they keep shooting
tongues cocked but i'm ready
hair tangled like a netting
eyes wing-tipped, hazardous
i walk into rooms already flexing
an armor
i can't rub holes into
i swell before they try
smiling
with both rows
of teeth

Ballads Us Girls Danced To*

Created from prom stories collected of Black girls in Madison, Connecticut

1.

                                        I

                                                        dress

up.   a
brief moment   the mirror
            a white
                    GOD   a wish
            in   Caucasian
confidence

                                                blonde hair and blue
eyes
stuck

                                                        in
                            focus

            a
                    mine   of
                        regret   I struggle

                                                with

                                                peace
                                                    bring me
what I deserve

2.

No one asked

expectation

to   hurt

I   a
current   a conversa-
tion   I
put   myself
in   waiting for   want   I
know   my   love
struggle

my body
the   balance
soul   sex

exhaust
all over

remind me
that I am

The first boy to call me beautiful

had hair like a kinked fist, walked
down the hallway, radius of curl
beckoning white hands he'd
allow. I'd watch a little
light in him dim. This,
a language us onlies have,
where no words need exist
at all.
Survival.
Head nod.

Mitchell was his name.
He came to our town escaping
a poor Harlem corner. Moved
in with a white family, started
playing lacrosse. Think
Fresh Prince meets
The Blind Side meets
other stories of brown boys
who could
never fit.

This, while I convinced myself
to like salad just for the Abercrombie
jeans hanging in my closet.
Pushed straight hair over
sodium hydroxide scabs.
The need to fit louder than
the burn crawling up my neck.

Most times, his friends,
no-lip white boys, spit
in my direction, then, messaged
me to ask what my mouth

might do, knowing they'd pass
me in hallways later
        laughing
              laughing
                    laughing.

Imagine my joy
looking down to see his name
lighting the phone, a new tone
ringing as blood pushed
and softened the Black
of my cheeks.

Ur beautiful

From the only boy who might understand
what those words mean.

but don't tell ne1[†] I said that, ok?

---

† ne1: a common shortening of the word "anyone," used for texting
and instant messenger

The Guilford Fair, 2008

I arrived suffocated.
Tight denim miniskirt,
marooned skin to September.

Thighs, goosebumped,
begging, as neon lights
gave body glitter a reason:

want was a joke
we were all learning to tell.
Emergency vehicles parked

so kids could play in them,
cherry-stained,
waving violent fingers

while underclassmen found
real danger, hid behind artisan
tents, muddied themselves

with liquor smuggled
in Gatorade bottles.
I watched like a hallway

anticipating Monday's
rumors, a spectator
against which poor decisions

bounced. I held them all,
not envious, but full
of stories, never mine.

Jackie, my ride home, walked
into the woods to make out
with her 3rd boy. I waited

stuffing cotton candy in my mouth
til the blue dug a grave in my molar.

Asha*

Created from prom stories collected of Black girls in Madison, Connecticut

at senior prom.

My date was

unseasoned food

For Shayla

Because we were the only two   in ballet class
who could not   blend into "nude"   tights

but could move on the two & four   &
her white mother   might've asked

my mother   about ways   to slick
a bun   out of kinks.   So, we were kin.

Even our brothers   played   in little league
together &   we kept the same cafeteria table

until high school when my hips grew out
like a pirouette   body tarred   like tap shoe.

          Always a barre between us.

I yearned   all   her yellow
her curls' bow   to gravity,

how she   danced   graceful
around my loud   everything.

My loud   everything   sitting quietly
as if to wait   its turn.

Zoë Mourns Her First

One look at his ruddy face
and you knew he drove a truck,
drank too much, cursed at his mother.
A bully some MTV movie imagined
and spat into our small town.

These are the boys I got
while girls like Jackie brought
boyfriends home for dinner,
pressed corsages into yearbooks.

Luxuries we dreamt
into old MASH games
and buried in lockers with the rest
of our teenage debris.

I wanted more,
and even a mean boy's lips
can blow dust off wonder,
teach the reckless business
of back seats, where I'd sneak
with him every Saturday,
attempting to memorize
the turbulence of his breath.

So much anger squatted
there, in the air around
his flayed syllables, claiming
space where apologies
should've been.

I thought the nights he held me
were worth the days he passed
in the hallway, not even a hello.

I thought the times he touched me
earned the times he struck, injury
ancillary to what I wanted
so badly to be tender.

White Boy Tells Me I'll Be Gone by 30

it's just that you are so much this popped collar of a boy repeats

smiling like he conquered something confident & without
mourning he credits

   how my laughter contemplates

         a cliff   my breath's loud bark

   surely, I'll vanish   if I continue to live all at once

junior year & I raised hell on my forearm razor marks passed
as cat scratches

       tiny

 evacuations of salt licked the tops of my thighs I already died

   allowed the boy   to grab me by the soft pink
of my lonely

   trembled next to him   while his fingers touched
   where I ached   poured

   me back   into an ocean

   as if Black isn't already a body   roaring

Hunger*

Created from prom stories collected of Black girls in Madison, Connecticut

everyone   white, weighed 100 pounds

    I
starved myself   perfect.
                           not one
ounce of

full

            I felt

silly   warped

inside and out

For Zoë

We looked   nothing alike   but
they could never tell us   apart

cuz our bodies cackled
down   hallways

hips scoffed   at Abercrombie jeans
lips   bloomed into   nobody's

bouquet   both of us
the only

but you my problem

your pressed hair's   stiff apology
how you leaned   in

let your friends   say *nigga*
kissed boys   under bleachers

didn't flinch when   they took
other girls   to prom

when you   laughed
you looked   around to see

who else   was watching
I'm sorry   I wanted   to hate you

didn't yet know   the difference
between   wanting to be seen

and wanting to fit

what cruel math, this survival

The First Saturday of June

I asked my mom to ask her friend if her son was free the first Saturday of June, to ask if he felt altruistic, if he wouldn't mind renting a tux and dancing awkwardly next to 582 sweating kids that looked nothing like him. He said yes. And no, I didn't get one of those elaborate promposals, but I've learned not to be gluttonous in my want. Thus, having a boy (with dimples like his) agree to be my date was enough.

In my world of *One Tree Hill*, *Degrassi*, and *Summerland*, touch seemed so easy it even reached out and nudged my expectation, every locker in every hallway seemed full of possibility: crumpled MASH games, origami fortune tellers, scratch paper "will-you-go-steadys". Sometimes I'd walk to the library and thumb the shelves in case my one true love and I reached for the same book. Those days, most of my experience with romance was just extending a hand to some nonexistent stranger, but seeing as I spent Junior Prom at the movies by myself watching *Something Borrowed*, I really tried this time. The scars on my arms had healed by then, and my gown, rose gold and draped over my body, moved like the ocean clinging to me as I emerged from it. And the star of the show, the bust, sparkled, too, like the ocean, but right as the sunset shakes it into a finale of mirrors.

I was beautiful that night, next to some handsome boy whose favor I was, who was too polite to touch me, and so we didn't dance at all. He sat with me kindly as the DJ played "We Are Young." And I left, not full, just satisfied, a gesture towards the same spine.

Fine, I'll Tell You the Truth

my expecta-

tion, a crum-

pled fortune

a stranger, I

Borrowed

i

left, not full, just the same

The Black Men outside the Waterfront Safeway Catcall Me

& I'm sure it's not me who they call for.
DC winters make any contact,
flickering lash, a fire to put your hands over.

They stand like barren trees,
crooked teeth shiver like hood castanets,
remind them of worlds other than corners.

I wonder who they have at home to be tender to,
if they paid the bill, if this small moment
of devotion runs like a furnace.

In this city of rush hours and new buildings,
of no one here is from here anymore,
even the air becomes brittle with lonely.
Maybe they yell *I love you* just to hear the echo.

For K

after Angel Nafis

One look at you they never knew;
you carried a religious thud, sister

A small dimness hostaged your sky;
that school paid you in mud, sister

Spectacle stomach, pageant chest—
they tried to dam that flood, sister

Occupied the tongue with a stillness;
silence punctured you like a stud, sister

Chose flight over death and still
you echo in this town, a dove, sister

No language for what we shared,
but between us, a kind of blood, sister

Zoë Eats a Man*

Created from prom stories collected of Black girls in Madison, Connecticut

Sorry

is

dominant
it

hook
anything

it

claim   to

grow

A
mean   jungle

with   black girl

less than

John Smith

I

crush   him   and

he

A   hole

of

hurt

A

kind of

sorry

can use

Let me   note

publicly   I'm

the idea of being desired

object   treated as

sex

They wanted

41

me

hidden   like

a   body

with

                                        fire,

    what hurt me

    was

    never

                                                human

        just   abuse

translated to

                            A

        bed

    I   realized

                                    that

you can use   anything
    if

                                                            you
kill it.

3

Vigilante

In the war against me
I am the fortress,
cold, standing.
Around me, a moat
that is also me,
running circles and licking dirt.
Cannons spitting
from the roof,
black as me,
exploding like me,
clapping through the air.

In the war, the nights are me
and the knights are me,
riding their strong, tired horses
whose hooves arpeggio the mud,
creating a song that is me.

My dance card is full;
soldiers keep coming
to offer their gentle hands:

Men who live in my building,
Whose daughters went to my school,
Whose daughter I am,
Who are 20 years my senior,
Who aren't men yet,
Who've signed my checks,
Who, against metro stations,
line themselves like artillery,
and whistle clean as exit wounds.

Of course my humanity hollowed;
mercy burned down
with all the other small towns.

The smoke? That's me, too.

"Why Are You So Extra?"

What else could I be but wild?	Two angry men slept inside my childhood	Dandelions convinced they were flowers
I stayed		Little wishes wasted everywhere
So many fists attempting to pull me from the root	I played at the edge of the busy road	I learned to fight by growing wide as seeds

How to Sweeten Lead

The uncle who made my dad's first
strawberry milkshake was
the same uncle who showed him
how to hold a gun

A 9-year-old slurping until his head turned
inside out, until he got a taste
for the color red, and the sugar dug
a grave for curiosity to rest

Whisky-slacked, his uncle claimed
a kitchen corner, took
it upon himself to teach
what mama was too afraid to:

> *It's cold out there, Son. Blood*
> *curdles once spilled, smells*
> *like pavement after rain, like*
> *even a rainbow could shoot*
> *over it and take you to the sky*
> *where real gold is*

A smaller version
of my father nodded,
his mouth too busy savoring
its own silence that he
had no choice but to swallow
every word

Origin of the Mistress

Cotton-calloused, I come
from women who knew too well
the wide vocabulary of hurt.

Who learned early the menace
of touch and replaced
"I love you's" with warnings

> *Don't be one of them fast girls*
> *Better cross those legs*
> *Cover your shoulders.*

But where is justice in that:
a body loved with fear
a body valued by its leash?

I'll free myself wild,
chew through leather,
howl without a moon.

Become my own moon.
Wax night.

Right Now, There Is a Man Depending on My Silence

I won't die

    without making
       your floorboards
          sing

     without taking
        with me

      the good
  silverware   your clean
         secrets

               your favorite hoodie
                  ragdolled
            over the same chair

     your obnoxious peace

    the drawers you keep

        your toys   party favors
        for

    the many colorful nameless
      guests

    when only the roaches
      left

you'll hear it

      just there
      underneath

    the filth

      of my   absence

your ego's hum

yes there

a dirge stretches

to the corners
like a fitted sheet
    soaked in sweat

        the purple
        walls

            floor to ceiling
            curtains their

                suggestive promises

                will no longer
                sustain

                    even the fresh lilies
                    you buy
                    every week

                    won't open

                    your carefully curated
                    everything

                        yes   Everything

                    you've touched

                will tell the truth.

Mistress

I don't get many Saturdays
but when I do, I'm your girl   lipsticked

my hand happily sweating in yours.
There are so many rivers between us:

Here, the Potomac moves its old skirt.
There, your wife pours her third glass.

I play dress-up in my daze,
wear scarves you bought in my hair,

convince you to give me a weekend.
Sometimes crumbs are all I need, I say,

smiling wide like a detonation.
You lick between my breasts

I look down   expecting rubble.
Hours pinned into expensive sheets

until the curtains wave their white flags.
In that apartment you painted

the color of Haiti, you sang with the barrel
of your mouth. I begged your old records

to swallow the ringing phone, for you
not to answer, to miss the flight—

I loved you. I thought it pardoned me.
Each apology, kissed into my forehead.

The sky still turned orange
from your quiet leaving.

The Black Men Aren't outside Safeway Today

No ballad No golden teeth Nor whistling gaps No ragged mutt warming the carriage of an abandoned shopping cart No chess set with missing rooks No sirens No lights Nor caution tape to redirect traffic away from the scream of cruor staining concrete like tomatoes kissing a bad joke No insistent *Hey, Miss Lady* interrupting my errands No need to ask *what happened?*

No flinching when I buy organic clementines

just remnants of someone's
yelling mouth I need
to clean from my shoes

Dissemblance

Gave no name for the siren
between my legs nor a siren
for the men who want
to be there.
No relief sounding
above her fallacy of wait.

She, who had me convinced
she married my father first,
like it wasn't before that:
father's nervous hands
making birds on lamp-lit walls.
Like she didn't recite scripture
into his neck. Like the room
wasn't red with breath,
then with mourning.

Fragmented faith, sin,
a sudden possibility,
a not-yet daughter
giving herself over
to a man, not-God,
disappearing beneath hymn.

This is how we birth rupture.
The hymen is not a promise, though
when broken it is said to stain
gentle things.

Can she tell?
When I say *virgin*, I mean
I have knelt before a body.
When I say *loss*, I mean
the blood is everywhere.

The back, its layered hunch,
into the parts of me that wept,
the heavy silence after,
a plague unto itself.
And when it was over,
a mess
no one taught me
to clean.

Critical Missing I

i. Name: *(for Seayauna)*

> She pins it to her chest
> like a brooch worn to some fancy
> mayoral dinner, and not the gray
> high school where she was
> last seen by her girls
>
> Those girls, who'd call
> 'cross halls, savoring
> the holiness of her
> name as if speaking
> in tongues, waiting for her
> arrival, her gallop,
> all limbs, this gangly,
> 14-year-old messiah
>
> Maybe
>
> they call her "Sea"
> 'cause she erodes mountains
> to sand with a smile;
> the loudest softest thing
>
> "See"
> praise her ember eyes
> their angry marvel
> at a shapeshifting city,
> shedding skin with each
> teenage year
>
> Or maybe
>
> they call her "Ana"

an abbreviated hosanna
the way all missing
Black girls
Are

ii. Missing From:

What is home
to a snake
that tires
even of
its own skin

I'd say
I was taken
from home
but home
hasn't claimed
me since
it stopped
goin' by
Chocolate City

It don't
sound alarms
for me no more
don't even
look

It just hiss
tell me *Go!*
twice
like it means it

iii. Last Seen:

On this southwest block,
decay crowds air with smoke
while men who'd squeeze
my cheeks when I was little
lick their lips as I walk by,
sprout wings and sing
love songs
through glassy eyes.

I learned to keep my head down
since turning 11.

I'm 14.

Last seen, you ask?
Only my shadow
would know.

iv. Time:

The sun bled everywhere I darkened
into the shadow of a poplar it was 1929
I became a widow it was 1960
the bus hum mothered me soothed
the calluses on my prayers it was 1985
church bells wept around us pallbearers
ushering in a white-gloved grief the sun
beat us all we stripped and leapt
into the river it was noon the cool wet grass
greeted us as we ran through midnight
yesterday offering tomorrow its hand
and I danced barefoot for the last—

v. Contact:

So many ways to lose
    a daughter, and

the hurt of an empty room be
    a mother itself
        a womb, haunted
        by fruit punch lip smackers,
        Big Sean posters; things
        her only loved thing
        loved, where
her only loved thing
rested her head

What rest does a mother's head have?
    She still picks up
    strawberry Pop-Tarts
        just in case

ends every conversation with
Call me if you see her

vi. Description of the Incident:

█ Metropolitan ████████████████████ public█
██
████████████████████████████████████, March
██████████████████████████████████████

████████████████████████████ a Black female██████████
██
███████████████████████ was last seen ████████████
██
██████████████████████

A

Spring, After a Year of Not Being Touched

Clouds suggest blue
after rain finally stops its tantrum.

Forsythia ornament mud, gold petals
flash tinsel against the gray.

March, again. Bare branches snarl at the sky
before, ultimately, giggling like shy girls

unable to keep their cool, sneeze color
everywhere until DC begins

to breathe easy and my dresses begin
to flirt with me from the closet. I imagine

our hemisphere leaning into sun,
thirsty to hear its sweet nothing.

The rush, sending this brief storm
to the tip of the Mason Dixon—

puddles everywhere begging for feet.
Feet everywhere looking
                              to jump.

"You Smell Like the Outside"

(→) Verb 1. As in, to ride sky home 2. As in, to stick to the air 3. As in, to open to spring, or 4. be opened by spring 5. to persuade the sun to hand over its extra hour

(→) Noun 1. As in, you, making the world generous 2. As in, bushes blushing yellow roses 3. As in, rock-rubbed palms turning into palm trees reaching for good weather, holding still birds, or 4. dragonflies or just 5. a shade of green, deep as kin

(→) Adj. 1. As in, Black: hopscotched and freeze-tagged and re-turned "It," touched, fragrant as if the day chose you 2. As in, wild: your hair, mud-mopped by play. 3. I bury my nose in it, and your laughter calls me strange 4. As in, your youth grows long instead of old 5. Alive: your beautiful skin keeps what the wind let go

What Singing Feels Like

I sing and sound
like all of them

the choir I am
haunts a bell
in my register

A voice contains
more than one body

sopranos loosen
the harmony
sheltering
in a skeleton

A song is
what arrival
sounds like

needs red carpet
to coax it out
from where it
holds shadows
like organs

shakes
the chandelier
well before
I open my mouth

I guess a voice
is hereditary   or
a voice bleeds

I learned soley
by being born

Ghost

I text my exes when I'm bored
because I like the drama
of bringing the dead back to life.
I mean, there's that Patrick Swayze movie,
and then MJ's "Thriller" video.
We, too, like the idea of gravedancing
just to see a limb reach longingly
for our ankles.

And what is living
if not for the recklessness that makes
mortuaries out of our chests,
the haunting of a good memory,
a man you already put down?

My mama's worried, knows
the habit I make of speaking to ghosts.
Say I need to go to church.
Say men there got more light
in their eyes. I say,
where's the fun in that?
I show the clean black of my shoulders
and attract men that only blossom
in a full moon.

The last one would never
be welcomed in a sanctuary.
Decorated his body with ink
til he the color of ash,
punched holes through his skin
just to make another exit.
I still dream
of falling into his mouth

just to be swallowed by something
not there tomorrow.

Take off the white sheet of this metaphor
and there is only a Black girl
accepting love from disappearing men.
Love, an apparition,
a cold wind, slamming door,
sweet boys hanging in tarnished photos,
plaguing my empty rooms.

And what is love if not a spirit
I exorcise from my own heart,
that never stays in one home,
that leaves home, that leaves me
to digest a different fairy tale,
where the girl is just happy
she made it out
alive?

Ode to the Hickey

Some call it childish,
result of being clumsy, eager,
not watching your mouth
or its mess.
Call it a silent *come here*
finishing
in a loud, deep purple.

When honest, it is
all breath, and spit, and now–
and now– the blood beneath
the surface, whispering.

A smaller me might have
worn scarves in summer
just to hide what my skin wanted,
when boys thought me too Black
to bloom a bruise.

Now I trace the edges
in the mirror,
thank all the boys
whose secret I was
for giving me a lie
to drown.
Gladly trading shame
for public side eyes,
wolf whistles,
wrapped like scarves
around my throat.

No garment compares
to the silk of a proud lover,
who claims me, shouts

against my neck a panting hue,
a pendant to proximity.

Dancing Boy on the Green Line Shares a Song with Me

> *Here.*

He passes his left earbud
& wires wishbone between us,
our cheeks pressed together
like siblings.

The best thing about Blackness
is the fictive kin: everyone
brother, sister, cousin,
a congregation
forming from bone.

The metro, full of witnesses,
their boring suits,
their quiet bodies,
but We
baptize in this
disruption of still.

Rejoice! all those times
We find our people
and too, find
      a miracle.

Aspirational Self-Portrait as Woman Gardening in a Wide-Brimmed Hat

The sun lay
heavy, like a child
too tired to walk. Fingertips
staccato soil as I lift light, like its mother,
in my wide-brimmed hat. Every day, and at
my will, sprouts rise luminous, hum backup
to an old record embellishing the the quiet air. No, I am not lonely here,
alone with my chores and my chorus of living things. If any lover
passes through, I feed him apple slices, 7UP cake, lemonade
before demanding to be left with my own plenty:

the tiny moons of mud
beneath my fingernails
my singing shoulders
my feast blooming
from everything
I buried.

Ghazal for Dorothy's Heart

white houses cleaned in Westport,
sturdy, cement spine grandmother

nine children, three bedrooms
no space for crying grandmother

boyfriend's knuckles after dinner,
plate lick, pucker, brine grandmother

at twelve, dad ran to the station, no shoes,
please confine him, grandmother

sunday coconut cake, no church,
but Kool-Aid: *we fine* grandmother

fat swallowed by her heart,
soft like a landmine grandmother

hospital bed and family respects
make death a punchline grandmother

never shared secret recipes, tough,
foot leather, flatline grandmother

I do bad all by myself—a bluff
I grew armor like your rind, grandmother

The Black Men outside the Waterfront Safeway Play Lil' Jon

Heads heavy with 1s and 2s,
they perch outside the grocery,
sucking teeth at new neighbors
rushing home with La Croix boxes.
Neighbors who don't make eye contact,
fearing what they might find
in the bassline of the men's brilliant irises.

One makes a hi-hat of spit on pavement
and, for a moment, I think a sword lily
could grow there, where his mouth spills.
Its vibrant skin reclaiming concrete.

When I walk by they call me *Miss Lady*,
as a father might call me by my name.
My chest blooms in unison with their speakers,
the familiarity of its incessant clap.

You'd think it a survival,
even as I walk into the store,
music fading to silence,
each brown face beckons a nod
as if to say:
We still hear it,
We still hear it,
We still hear.

Who Answers the Questions My Loneliness Asks

- Highway static fogging apartment windows
- Police sirens waving red hands
- Lovers' metronoming against the wall
- Brothers calling out from balconies
- New ancestors flooding news streams
- Cicadas whispering back to a lawnmower
- A jackhammer singing its rebuttal
- A neighbor pointing at my marigolds
- Grandpa celebrating his 91st
- The drunk man preparing his afternoon sermon
- Dad calling now more than ever
- A city's new refusal
- A nation's old diagnosis
- Watering my dead flowers
- Speaking of what left in the present tense

On Disappearing

Look!
the men
crowd corners,
gather like
anomalies
bloomed,
a constant
spring, thaw
what tried
to take them.

They clap
their hands
to Go-Go,
and embers
leap
from their palms
to emphasize
the point,
signal
the choir
for when one
don't show up;
the matches
of their fingers
strike,
lighting memories
like loosies.

//

And this is what I excavate in the minute it takes to walk by.
I, still smelling like the small town I came from, still staring
the way my mother taught me not to, but they're all uncles,

sweat and father's shoulders.

Certainly, their mamas worked alongside their mamas.
Certainly, I've sat next to their sons on the train.
Certainly, they are my cousins, kissing teeth   at falling buildings,
pouring liquor for the fallen people, buried only to grow
into our own faces.

My people stubborn; die soon and become heirlooms,
legacies screaming like streetlights. Tell you to go home
the same way they tell you to come here.

And there:

salt water, summer tar, slow dance,
bible verse, birthmark, bad temper,
flat tire, flat line, funeral feast.
Sunflowers opening wide like a fire.

Acknowledgments

Breakbeat Poets Vol. 2: Black Girl Magic: "Ode to an Almost First Kiss"

Gargoyle Magazine: "Ghost"

Split This Rock's *The Quarry*: "The Black Men outside the Waterfront Safeway Play Lil' Jon"

Arlington Literary Journal: "My Mother Once Flattened My Father's Tires," "Sugar," "Ode to the Hickey," "The Black Men outside the Waterfront Safeway Catcall Me'

Southern Indiana Review: "The Groomsman"

Sundog Lit: "On Disappearing"

The Rumpus: "Zoë Eats a Man," "The first boy to call me beautiful," "The Black Men outside the Waterfront Safeway Serenade Me"

TORCH: "Vigilante"

The Adroit Journal: "Critical Missing II"

Frontier: "Aspirational Self-Portrait as Woman Gardening in a Wide-brimmed Hat"

Muzzle Magazine: "Why Are You So Extra?", "You Smell Like the Outside"

So much gratitude . . .

For Maya, Aricka, Jameka, and the rest of the Haymarket Books team. For poetry godparents Kevin, Dan, & Mahogany: you all believed this collection into being . . . even before I did. Y'all are true dream engines. Thank you.

For the communities who have showed me the kind of artist I want to be: Center for Creative Youth at Wesleyan University, Split This Rock, DC Youth Slam Team, Shout Mouse Press, The Grind, Tin House, The Watering Hole & Cave Canem. I am forever a student of yours.

For Toi Derricotte and Cornelius Eady, always. No amount of gratitude feels like enough.

For the people who've put their hands on these poems: Ariana Benson, Raina León, Joladé Olusanya, Peter deGraft-Johnson, Tanatsei Gambura, Courtney Conrad, Keri Mosuro, Len Lawson, Be Manzini, Nick Makoha, Raymond Antrobus, Malika Booker, Roger Robinson, Dante Micheaux, Quenton Baker, Luther Hughes, Kim Marshall, Teri Elam, Jari Bradley, Abdul Ali, Rachael Uwada Clifford, de'Angelo Dia, Dave Harris, Christopher Rose, Rage Hezekiah, Malcolm H. Tariq, Nicholas Goodly, mace dent johnson, Kush Thompson, Sacha Marvin Hodges, Safia Elhilo, Kyle Dargan, Rasheed Copeland, Gabriel Ramirez, Elizabeth Acevedo, Clint Smith, Julian Randall, Sasha Debevec-Mckenney, Malik Thompson, Marissa Davis, Michelle Hulan, Khadijah Queen, James O'Bannon, Phylise Smith, Kimberly Reyes, Toney Lombardi & Loisa Fenichell. What generous alchemy you've spun on my work. Thank you.

For Camila Dechalus, Lee France, Charles Walker, Beatrice Greenberg, Dele Amon, Izzy Rode, David McCamish, Frankie

Alicea, Chelsea Iorlano, Lisa Lumeya, Nathan Podziewski, & Rachel Zwick: dear friends of my heart and mind, ever generous with your love and with yourselves. Thank you for all the ways you give my spirit its second wind.

For Alyssa Ahern, Megan Ahern, Kate Gladstone, Rebecca Rubinstein, Kimmy Megargee, Hannah Clorite & Sophie Zinser— high school wasn't all bad. If we are still in touch, or if we let time do what it does, you all saved my life with laughter alone. Endless gratitude and love for all of you.

For all the Black girls who attend or have attended Daniel Hand High School. For all the Black girls who survive or have survived being the only. For all the Black girls who survive or have survived, or didn't—*I love you joy is coming.*

For my family: Mom, Dad, Kristian, Nathalie, Maya, Brendan, Grandpa, Nana, all the cousins, uncles n' aunties. None of this exists without you, the mess in your brilliant love & your love.

For all my people, the muse of our ghosts, our daily masterclass in swag and still here. We: present tense. I love you.

& you, dear reader, for your time and trust. Thank you for taking this journey with me.

Notes

* The prom erasure series featuring poems, "Ballads Us Girls Danced To," "Asha," "Hunger," and "Zoë Eats a Man," were created from actual accounts of Black girls from my hometown, Madison, Connecticut. Over the spring and summer of 2020, when many of us had nothing to do except be online, I developed the series in order to use social media for a purpose that felt more generative than draining. The process would prove to be just as spiritually generative as it was artistically.

I started by interviewing Black girls who attended high school at the same time I did. However, though we shared time in school we mostly varied in graduation year, social group, and ethnicity. As a young person, I saw these differences between us as barriers to connection, to coalition. Admittedly, I even judged some for presenting too "assimilated" or "passive" to the overt injustices of our environment. With time, I've realized that I was ignorant to the depths of their hurt and that my judgement, too, was a white supremacist fallacy that kept us apart and made our survival lonely.

Why prom? Because prom was the happy ending to every teenage movie from which we were erased. It is the pink ribbon tied around the high school experience. The celebratory exit from the awful, awkward, and liminal. The glamorous entry into what feels like "the world." Hilariously, the reality is: prom REALLY ain't that deep. But, between the wildly public promposals and goal weights, not loading the moment with meaning felt impossible. And politics, too, nestled themselves deep inside of that meaning, asking: Who got asked? Who stayed home? Who felt beautiful? Who were told that they were beautiful? Who had a good time? These were the questions from which I based my interviews.

I reached out to my distant classmates via Facebook and Instagram, collected their written or audio-recorded accounts, transcribed them as needed, and got to work, keeping each participant anonymous (using aliases in the written text).

Once drafts were complete, I gathered us all on Zoom to show the pieces and answer any questions. However, there were no questions, and through simple "catching up" and "checking in," the space quickly evolved into a sanctuary from which healing and understanding poured. I walked into this project expecting to get a few poems. I emerge from the work with a book and section of what has become an entire blooming sisterhood.

About the Author

Alexa Patrick is a poet and singer from Connecticut. She is a Cave Canem Fellow and Tin House alumna. Her work has been published in *The Quarry*, *Arlington Literary Journal*, *CRWN Magazine*, and *The Breakbeat Poets Vol. 2: Black Girl Magic*. *Remedies for Disappearing* is her first collection.

About Haymarket Books

Haymarket Books is a radical, independent, nonprofit book publisher based in Chicago. Our mission is to publish books that contribute to struggles for social and economic justice. We strive to make our books a vibrant and organic part of social movements and the education and development of a critical, engaged, and internationalist Left.

We take inspiration and courage from our namesakes, the Haymarket Martyrs, who gave their lives fighting for a better world. Their 1886 struggle for the eight-hour day—which gave us May Day, the international workers' holiday—reminds workers around the world that ordinary people can organize and struggle for their own liberation. These struggles—against oppression, exploitation, environmental devastation, and war—continue today across the globe.

Since our founding in 2001, Haymarket has published more than nine hundred titles. Radically independent, we seek to drive a wedge into the risk-averse world of corporate book publishing. Our authors include Angela Y. Davis, Arundhati Roy, Keeanga-Yamahtta Taylor, Eve Ewing, Aja Monet, Mariame Kaba, Naomi Klein, Rebecca Solnit, Olúfẹ́mi O. Táíwò, Mohammed El-Kurd, José Olivarez, Noam Chomsky, Winona LaDuke, Robyn Maynard, Leanne Betasamosake Simpson, Howard Zinn, Mike Davis, Marc Lamont Hill, Dave Zirin, Astra Taylor, and Amy Goodman, among many other leading writers of our time. We are also the trade publishers of the acclaimed Historical Materialism Book Series.

Haymarket also manages a vibrant community organizing and event space in Chicago, Haymarket House, the popular Haymarket Books Live event series and podcast, and the annual Socialism Conference.

Available from Haymarket Books

All the Blood Involved in Love, Maya Marshall

Black Queer Hoe, Britteney Black Rose Kapri

The BreakBeat Poets Vol. 2: Black Girl Magic, ed. by Mahogany L. Browne, Idrissa Simmonds, and Jamila Woods

Build Yourself a Boat, Camonghne Felix

Can I Kick It?, Idris Goodwin

Citizen Illegal, José Olivarez

I Remember Death by Its Proximity to What I Love, Mahogany L. Browne

Lineage of Rain, Janel Pineda

Mama Phife Represents, Cheryl Boyce-Taylor

Milagro, Penelope Allegria

The Patron Saint of Making Curfew, Tim Stafford

Rifqa, Mohammed El-Kurd

Super Sad Black Girl, Diamond Sharp

There Are Trans People Here, H. Melt

Too Much Midnight, Krista Franklin

CPSIA information can be obtained
at www.ICGtesting.com
Printed in the USA
JSHW081520090523
41454JS00002B/3